How to Write a Funny Speech...

How to Write a Funny Speech...

for a Wedding, Bar Mitzvah, Graduation & Every Other Event You Didn't Want to Go to in the First Place

**CAROL LEIFER &
RICK MITCHELL**

CHRONICLE BOOKS
San Francisco

Library of Congress Cataloging-in-Publication Data

Names: Leifer, Carol, author. | Mitchell, Rick J., author.
Title: How to write a funny speech... : for a wedding, bar
    mitzvah, graduation & every other event you didn't want
    to go to in the first place / Carol Leifer & Rick Mitchell.
Description: San Francisco : Chronicle Books, 2025.
Identifiers: LCCN 2024032489 | ISBN 9781797232232
    (hardcover)
Subjects: LCSH: Public speaking. | Wit and humor. |
    Speechwriting. | Humorous recitations.
Classification: LCC PN4129.15 .L44 2003 | DDC 808.5/
    1--dc23/eng/20240809
LC record available at https://lccn.loc.gov/2024032489

Manufactured in China.

MIX
Paper | Supporting
responsible forestry
FSC™ C008047

Design by Wynne Au-Yeung.

10 9 8 7 6 5 4 3 2 1

Chronicle books and gifts are available at special quantity discounts to corporations, professional associations, literacy programs, and other organizations. For details and discount information, please contact our premiums department at corporatesales@chroniclebooks.com or at 1-800-759-0190.

Chronicle Books LLC
680 Second Street
San Francisco, California 94107
www.chroniclebooks.com

For my wife, Lori,
and our son, Bruno.

Carol

To my wife, Barbara, and
our daughter, Katherine,
for your unwavering love
and support.

Rick

Foreword

I wish I knew how to write a Funny Foreword. So I'm not even going to try.

However, I can certainly say that Carol and Rick have written a masterpiece that can come to your rescue when you have to give a (gulp!) speech for any occasion.

I might add that this is also a Funny Masterpiece.

Along with admiring their sage advice, I found myself laughing out loud.

—CAROL BURNETT

Introduction

So you agreed to speak at someone's event. But now you're freaking out because you have to actually write a speech. It's very daunting and we can certainly relate. We had to write an entire book on how to write speeches. At least you don't have to do that.

A cloud of anxiety envelops you. "What the hell am I gonna say? I know *him*; he was my fraternity brother. But her? Not at all. And it's been quite a while since we've seen each other. Look, I'm pretty funny with my friends, but in front of a room full of strangers? How many shots of tequila is it going to take to get me up there in front of all those people and actually *do this*?"

Public speaking. It remains the number one fear for the average person. And with the advent of phones that can record *everything*, the ubiquitous threat of forever looms large. What used to be a "story" among the relatives ("Wow! Aunt Jen said you really ate it last night with that toast you made at Steve and Marsha's wedding!") has become a link that's *everywhere*! Oh, you weren't thinking about this being recorded?

Did you just come out of a cave? Pressure's on now more than ever.

Rest assured, we (Carol and Rick) have witnessed the drama firsthand. God-awful speeches that were not only humiliating for the speechmakers but also really put a damper on entire events. What were supposed to be heartfelt, humorous tributes turned out to be unmitigated disasters. If only there had been a book written by two experienced stand-ups and television writers who could have shown them the way . . .

Now there is. After years of watching countless speech-givers make all the rookie mistakes and fail epically, we're here to help! From start to finish, we're going to show you how to create an appropriate, sincere, and, most importantly, *funny* tribute that will be the talk of your event. Hey! Instead of entering a state of paralysis over the disastrous speech going up on YouTube, you'll be the one endlessly sharing the link, glowing from all the positive comments and praise from family and friends.

Getting Started

As we begin to craft your speech, there are a bunch of signposts to be aware of. These essential factors are the foundation of a good speech: the length, the where, and the tone of what you want to say. Keep these in mind as you sit down to write.

Keep It Under Five

This just may be the most important piece of advice we're going to give you. Your speech should time out to five minutes or under. Nothing ruins a wedding quicker than a *looonnnggg* speech. It's a crowd killer, and people will never forgive you for as long as you live. Sorry if we're being a little intense here, but you have no idea how many people blather on and on obliviously in their speeches, not reading the room. There's a reason "More is more" did not become a saying.

So keep it at five minutes max. If it's a very intimate wedding with a small number of guests, feel free to loosen the reins and speak a little more. But remember! The Gettysburg Address was 272 words, and it lasted around two minutes. There's a reason Lincoln's on the penny.

Signs Your Speech Is Too Long

- You hear crying, and it's not a baby.

- You get a standing ovation after you say, "In conclusion . . ."

- You think people are laughing at your speech, but the guests are actually watching cat videos on their phones.

- The happy couple is already on their honeymoon.

- You're getting calls from collection agencies for the tuxedo you rented but never returned.

- The bride's bouquet is now dried flowers.

- Your phone has updated twice.

- The music starts to play over your speech like it does at awards shows.

- You've been invited to the couple's vow renewal.

Location, Location, Location!

Where is your speech taking place? This is one of the biggest factors to take into consideration before drafting your speech. Yes, believe it or not, the number one rule of real estate also figures into this area—location, location, location.

Will your speech take place somewhere formal? Or is it at a bar downtown? Will it be at somebody's home?

One size does not fit all. The speech you deliver is always tied to its surroundings. Gushing to your sorority sister at her engagement party is one thing at a funky watering hole after a long night of partying, but quite another at her parents' tony country club. Factoring in your setting is crucial. So before writing *anything*, find out the "where."

The "when" of the "where" is something to consider too. A speech at a bar at midnight with the best man buying rounds is going to be vastly different from a speech at a bar before lunch at noon, with just mimosas being served. So figure in the time of day and what seems appropriate given the hour.

The "when" and "where" are critical: They dictate the overall tone. Which leads us to possibly the second-biggest mistake people make when giving a speech: using profanity—a lot of it. A good rule of thumb is to picture yourself giving your speech in front of Aunt Nancy and Uncle Bob. If you can visualize it without her pearls exploding or his toupee boomeranging across the room, you're on the right track. (More on that in the "Keep It Classy!" section.)

Look, if it makes you more at ease, write your first draft the way it feels most natural, f-bombs and all. But then go back through it and take out anything you wouldn't want to say in front of someone who thinks they're actually there for bingo night. We think it'll become clear to you exactly what we've discovered in our many collective years of doing stand-up: A lot of the time, profanity is a crutch. Challenge yourself by coming up with some alternatives to swearing. You'll be surprised to find that whatever you come up with is usually full of much more personality and more interesting than what you had before.

Another piece of advice that we've gleaned from the stand-up world: Always be ready to pivot. Meaning, maybe you were told that your speech was for just you and your buddies, but then at the last minute, some older family members were invited. You might have to get out that phone and start editing, because Grandma's compression socks might lose their elastic after hearing that her grandson used to get high on Molly and climb into the chimp habitat at the zoo just to "show those hairy mofos who's boss."

Keep It Classy!

To reiterate, no swearing. (Note: This all goes out the window if it's just you and your friends. The advice here is for a mixed-crowd, all-ages event.)

"But, Rick and Carol, I can get everybody to laugh when I use the f-word."

We bet you can. The f-word is pretty funny. But imagine you're at a wedding. Imagine you're in front of mothers and fathers and grandparents and *kids*? Not appropriate.

"But—"

No buts. Except the word *butt*. That's fine. But no swearing. Now shut the F up about it.

This rule also applies to nonverbal swearing. No middle finger. No doing inappropriate things with the microphone. No dry humping anyone. You're wearing a tux! You're wearing a gown that maxed out your credit card! That should indicate the importance of this event.

And keeping it classy means you're not going to touch certain topics.

You probably know all sorts of stories about the bride and/or groom. Like that time the groom and his ex-girlfriend did it in the back of your car. Or the time the bride had a threesome with your brother and his friend. Or even the time the bride, the groom, his ex-girlfriend, and your brother had a foursome in the back of your car. Please stop letting people use the back of your car.

These stories are probably hilarious but completely inappropriate at a wedding. Again, this is the bride and groom's day. They've just pledged to spend the rest of their lives together, so the last things they want to hear about are their spouse's ex-partners, adventures with strippers, or weeklong drug binges.

"But, Rick and Carol, the groom is a big drinker. It's, like, his thing. Everybody, even his family, knows this about him, and even they joke about it with him."

Well then, we would say it sounds like your friend has a problem, and he needs to get help. But also, yes, this would be an instance where it would be okay to crack a joke or two. Even other edgy topics might be okay if you approach them carefully with innuendo and subtlety. But be careful, and use discretion. Always better to err on the side of caution.

You may have just read this section and thought, "Duh." But you'd be surprised how many wedding speakers do these very dumb things. Don't make that mistake.

GETTING-STARTED TIPS

To recap:

- ☐ Keep it short and sweet.

- ☐ Think about the "where" and "when."

- ☐ Keep it classy! You're most likely giving your speech to a mixed crowd, so keep it G-rated.

The Beginning

Plain and simple, the beginning is the hardest part. The beginning means you actually have to sit down and start writing. Nobody looks forward to putting together their speech; that is a universal truth.

The number one mistake that people make right out of the gate is *not introducing themselves and telling the crowd their relationship to the honoree*. This is a key element to the beginning of your speech and, honestly, the easiest part, because how hard do you have to work to come up with this nugget? When a speech-giver doesn't tell the guests their relationship to the honoree up front, the bulk of the speech becomes an episode of *Dateline* for the guests.

"Is this a relative of some kind?"

"Is this an old friend or a recent one?"

"Is this someone who possibly stumbled into the wrong ballroom at the venue?"

It's so easy.

"I'm Louise, Cara's aunt on her mother's side, and we've been close since she was a little girl."

"I'm Jake, Ben's bunkmate for seven summers from Camp Tonawanda."

"Hi, I'm Louise. Can someone please tell me, am I at the Hyatt Regency or the Hyatt Place? Is this the Silverstein wedding?"

So don't let the crowd wondering endlessly "Who the hell is this?" ruin your speech. Let people know right away why you're special enough that you made the cut and were asked to speak.

Another great element that feels natural at the beginning of a speech is talking about how you first met the person. If it's your friend from college, tell the crowd about your first encounter in your poli-sci class or maybe just hanging out on the quad. If it's a family member, talk about your first recollection of them—like how your consciousness came to when your older brother found it humorous to tickle you until you peed your pants when you were five years old. Starting with this "way back" perspective sets you up nicely to move forward and, hopefully, get some early laughs in the process.

For example, at Carol's fortieth birthday party, her best friend since fifth grade, Cathy, made a speech. Right up top, she divulged their funny "how we met." Every day in the school lunchroom, she saw Carol buying her sandwich and ice cream both at the same time. Confused and a bit perturbed at watching Carol eat a slightly melted ice cream bar at the end of every lunch, Cathy walked over to Carol and said, "Have you ever thought about buying your ice cream *after* you've eaten your sandwich?" And so started a lifelong friendship. Many in the audience recognized this same quality about Carol through the years.

Rick, at his friend Ryan's wedding, told the story of meeting Ryan at their college orientation. When they were all eating breakfast in the dining commons, Rick noticed "this guy eating a bowl of dry cereal. And he had a cup of milk to drink, but with ice in it." Rick thought, "This guy might be weirder than me; I gotta meet him." Guests really appreciate stories like these—they tell volumes about the person you're toasting.

On the day of your speech, you should make sure to ask if somebody is going to introduce you. Normally, someone other than the honoree will get up there and say, "Okay, everybody! It's time to hear some speeches from some special folks." Usually, this will do you the favor of getting the crowd settled down and ready to listen. Trust us, it will make for a much better speech if someone is kind enough to do the honors of introducing you. If you go it alone out there—*clink, clink, clink!* on your champagne glass—it's not gonna be pretty.

THE BEGINNING TIPS

To recap:

☐ **Let the crowd know who you are and your relationship to the honoree.**

☐ **Share with the guests the story of how you first met.**

☐ **Before or at the event, ask if you are going to be introduced.**

The
Middle

Now let's get into the meat of your speech. What? Maybe later? Fear not! We're going to share a little trick with you that we both use when sitting down to write is the last thing we want to do. Tell yourself you're going to write for fifteen minutes only. After that, you are free to not write a single word more. And the funny thing is, we've both never gotten up and bailed after the allotted fifteen minutes. Once you sit down to do it, you'll be surprised that it's not as horrible as you imagined. Try it! It just might work for you like it has for us.

Okay, what should you write? The middle part of your speech, after you've introduced yourself and whom you're talking about, should be filled with personal stories. These are the *gold* of speech writing. Why? Because you want your speech to stand apart from everybody else's. The easiest way to guarantee your speech racks up views on the web is by sharing what nobody else has: *your stories*!

A good way to conjure up these stories is to think about the following:

- If you had to tell the funniest story about this person, what would it be? Did it involve you in some way?

- What's the best thing about this person's personality? What's the weirdest?

- What's the most outrageous thing this person's done?

- What's the most loving and generous gesture you've seen this person make?

Basically, if you were sitting at a bar and a stranger asked you to tell them about this person, what stories would come to mind?

And by the way, it's not cheating to ask other people (ideally friends and not strangers, don't be weird) for qualities that come to mind when they think of this person. It's not even cheating to ask them for stories too. As long as you give them credit if they ask for it ("Lizzie told me this story that completely sums up Evan . . ."), it's totally legit. And, hey, *they're* not getting their ass up there. Remind them of that if they give you a hard time!

Things to Remember

Work with What You Got

You're obviously going to know some people better than others, so the amount of information you have about the honoree may vary. Even if you do know them well, you may have trouble thinking of things.

Rick ran into this problem with his college friend Frank. He racked his brain but found it very difficult to think of things about him. In fact, the one thing that kept coming to mind was that he was the nicest person in the world. Everyone loved him, and you'd be hard-pressed to find anyone who'd say anything negative about him. Now, that's great if you're Frank. But not great if you're trying to write a funny speech about him.

So what do you do in this case? Best to deal with this type of problem by acknowledging it. There's still material here! Rick ended up making a joke about how nice Frank was. He said he was a little too nice, which probably meant he was hiding something. Like a body.

It's about the Couple, Stupid!

Carol recently went to a wedding where the father of the bride's speech was devoted entirely to the extraordinary achievements of his daughter. Basically, a reading of his accomplished daughter's résumé. *She graduated from this Ivy League school, her grade point average was a 4.0, she was at the top of her medical-school class*, and blah, blah, blah, on and on. It was embarrassing. So bad it became the talk of the line at valet parking when the wedding was over. The guests were so put off by it. "Was this a wedding or a job fair?" was actually overheard.

So, parents? Remember, this is a day about your child finding the love of their life. And as proud of them as you are as an individual, that's not what the wedding, or any other occasion, is about. Even if it's a graduation, the detailed facts and minutiae of their triumphs are not what's important. What's important is that you speak from the heart about this very special person or couple.

"It's about the couple" also means it's not about *you*. This is another huge mistake when giving a speech: talking all about yourself. Guests want to know your connection to the honoree, sure, but keep it about the person or people being celebrated.

Avoid Platitudes

What are platitudes? Go to the greeting cards
section of any store and read the cards for whatever
occasion you're writing the speech for. Or google
"_____ Wishes."

"Wishing you many blessings on your special day."

"Best of luck on your new beginnings!"

"Your someday is here. Enjoy!"

"This is the greatest love the world has ever seen."

Stuff that is usually embroidered on a pillow at HomeGoods is a solid point of reference.

Don't get us wrong: A well-worn sentiment here and there is fine, but we've heard speeches filled with one cliché after another, and you could see all the eyes in the audience glazing over.

Just the Facts, Ma'am

Little things mean a lot in a speech. And if it means devoting a small amount of time to getting the details right, do it.

For instance, are you using the person's preferred pronouns? Is their name pronounced MAY-gun, or is it MEG-un? How do you say their last name properly? You know how you feel when someone says *your* name wrong? Well, picture you're the bride on your big day and that happens. Insert her glaring look here.

Is Ed her father or her stepfather? Might be a small matter to you, but a huge one to the family at the event.

Is this the groom's fourth or fifth marriage? Actually, maybe that's a detail you can leave out altogether.

And if a story you're planning on telling feels a little fuzzy to you, check with friends. They might even add a tidbit that you didn't know.

If you feel like you need some help with your stories and how to make them a little funnier, read on.

Adding In the Funny

You're here because you don't have the cojones to fake
food poisoning so that you won't have to give this
speech to begin with. But you're also here because you
want your speech to be funny. Who doesn't want to hear
"Funny!" as you return to your seat at the affair?!

A good way to start to inject some humor into your
speech is to think of five attributes of the person you're
going to talk about. And the attributes you choose are
even better if most of them are universal. Meaning,
hopefully everyone else attending this event who knows
this person will recognize these same qualities. Before
you start, make a list of attributes that you can refer to
during the writing process.

We'll use Rick's expertise here, from a speech he gave at
the wedding of his best friend, Charlie. Here's what Rick
wrote for Charlie's five attributes.

- Wears tight-fitting clothes

- Terrible dancer

- Unusually small ears

- Sicilian

- A bit vain

So let's start with number one, wearing tight-fitting
clothes. It's one of the first things Rick thinks of when
he pictures Charlie: white T-shirts that are way too
small for him.

One way to make things funny is by exaggerating.
In reality, Charlie probably wears medium-size T-shirts
instead of large. Saying that is not really funny by
itself, so we play it up. Let's say he wore a smaller
size. How about a small? Even smaller. Extra small?
Keep going. Kids' size? Go smaller; we're almost there!
Baby size? Boom!

We're going to say Charlie wears baby shirts.

"Charlie is known to wear shirts that are way too
small for him. To this day, he actually still wears
his baby clothes."

Not bad, but it could be better. So now we start
brainstorming about baby clothes. What kinds of
clothes do babies wear? Onesies. Shirts that say
"I Love My Mommy."

Now we're going to think about where you get baby
clothes. The first thing that popped into Rick's head
was babyGap.

"Charlie is known to wear shirts that are way too small
for him. He actually shops at babyGap."

The only other thing he did to this joke was to set up a
comparison. So the final joke was this:

"Charlie is known to wear shirts that are way too small
for him. Growing up, we all shopped at the Gap. Charlie
shopped at babyGap."

So he took the core observation, that Charlie wears small shirts, and exaggerated it to the extreme. If you're overwhelmed, don't worry. You may not be able to make these connections right away. It takes practice. So let's practice more! Today's Wordle can wait.

Another description on the list was the fact that Charlie is a terrible dancer, and his bride-to-be, Rachel, is actually a dance-team coach. The observation was already amusing on its own:

"Isn't it interesting that Rachel is the coach of a college dance team, yet Charlie is the worst dancer on earth?"

Then, realizing that Charlie would actually have to dance shortly after this speech, Rick ended up tweaking this a little bit:

"Rachel is the coach of a college dance team. She teaches people how to dance. And as you'll see in a little bit, she hasn't had a chance to give Charlie a lesson yet."

Let us assure you, Rick did not come up with these jokes immediately. It really took some thinking to get them to that point. Some jokes may take longer than others to write. Here's an example. . . .

Shall we move on to "unusually small ears"? Wait, what? You didn't hear me?

Highlighting this physical detail seemed like something that should really work. Anyone who knew Charlie certainly would be in on this joke. The only problem was that Rick felt a bit out of gas. He tried writing jokes about Charlie's ears being so small that he couldn't hear anybody, but these zingers weren't zinging. After numerous attempts, he eventually just gave up on thinking of anything on this subject.

Then, on the day of the wedding, Rick decided to take one more stab at the unused topics on his list. For instance, he had made a list for Rachel, even though he clearly did not know her as well as he knew Charlie. And he'd written that Rachel once modeled in a magazine. Then he started imagining Charlie modeling for a magazine too. And then it came to him . . . what if Charlie had been a model for *Unusually Small Ears Magazine*?! Rick then tried to take the joke one step further. If Charlie were to model for something, what would be worse/funnier than a magazine? Brochure? Flyer? Pamphlet? And right when Rick thought of "pamphlet," he remembered those pamphlets that you find in doctors' offices. Wait! What if he made "unusually small ears" a medical condition? So this is the joke Rick ultimately wound up with:

"It's no surprise that Rachel looks fantastic today. She even once modeled in a magazine. Some of you may not know this, but Charlie also did some modeling. He appeared in a medical pamphlet for an affliction known as 'unusually small ears.'"

Rick finally got to the joke, but it took some time. And he's a professional comedy writer, for God's sake. So be patient with yourself.

By the way, can we go back to the small-ears joke for a minute? To us, this kind of joke is one to strive for at a wedding. Not only does it tease Charlie in a fun way, but it also flatters the bride. Notice how Rick threw in the compliment that she looks fantastic? Of course you did; you're very observant. So he was able to make her feel good by using her modeling as a setup to the punch line about Charlie's small ears. Rachel's happy that Rick pointed out how beautiful she looks. And the guests are happy that the joke was both nice and funny. And Charlie's happy, because he couldn't hear the insult on account of his unusually small ears.

THE MIDDLE TIPS

To recap:

- [ ] **Start by trying to list five personal attributes about the person—a good path to humor.**

- [ ] **Personal stories! About *them*! About the two of you together! That's the gold.**

- [ ] **Don't talk about yourself unless it's in relation to the honoree.**

- [ ] **Parents? Don't make your speech an obnoxious reading of your kid's résumé.**

- [ ] **Don't use clichés.**

- [ ] **No detail is too small to get right.**

Now let's look at a series of real speeches and see what worked well and what could have been better.

Rick's Speech for Charlie and Rachel's Wedding

Should we take a look at the speech that Rick wrote for Charlie and Rachel's wedding? Of course we should. Pay attention to how he ultimately incorporated all the jokes he crafted in "Adding In the Funny."

Carol = blue
Rick = brown

I'm so happy to be here to celebrate the wedding of Harley and Rachel. Sorry . . . Charlie and Rachel. Whatever, you know who I'm talking about.

First line, starting out funny.

For those of you who don't know me, my name is Rick, and I'm the best man. I first met Charlie when I was in third grade. I had just moved to Novato, California, from New Jersey. I was very nervous on the first day of school because I didn't know anyone. But during recess, Charlie asked if I wanted to join his football game. I did, and I sure as hell was grateful that he asked. (And please know I didn't use the word *hell* back in third grade.)

Sweet story about how Rick and Charlie met. The more details you include, the better.

So now I can say that I've known Charlie longer than any other friend . . . who I can't get rid of. Trust me, I've tried. I've changed phone numbers . . . identities . . . entered witness protection. I just can't shake the guy.

Charlie, you have no idea how long I've waited for this. I feel that everything I've done in the past has culminated in this moment right here . . . where I get to make fun of you.

A lot of people think Charlie is annoying. I won't say if that's true or not, but I will say that sometimes he calls telemarketers while they're having dinner.

Charlie and Rachel are Sicilian, which means before they were married they were already a family.

There are a lot of stereotypes about Sicilians. We all know them. But I know better than to make a joke about them. It's dangerous. They might put a horse head in my bed. Or make me eat a spicy meatball.

Anyone else think it's weird not to see Charlie in a small white T-shirt? That's his thing. As small as possible, right? Growing up, we all shopped at the Gap. Charlie shopped at babyGap.

Michael, Charlie's father, is here. Thank you for a wonderful rehearsal dinner last night. I'm sure a lot of you know that Michael worked for PG&E, Pacific Gas and Electric. That's very different than being a fireman, what Charlie does. Although Charlie does experience blackouts. And he has a lot of gas.

Rachel's father is here too. I don't really know him at all. But I saw the house you were kind enough to purchase for Charlie and Rachel, so I'd like to ask your permission now to marry your other daughter. Or your son. I don't care who. I'm very low on funds.

Rachel's dad bought them the most beautiful house. But the funny thing is, he didn't buy them any furniture. Have you ever seen a million-dollar house with no furniture? It looks like they've been robbed.

Obviously, I'm kidding. Can we get Rachel's dad a drink, please? But give him the glass without any liquid in it. See how that feels? Buy them some furniture.

And how about Rachel—doesn't she look beautiful? Some of you may not know this, but Rachel actually did some modeling. She appeared in *Maxim* magazine, quite the official "hot" stamp of approval. Charlie also did some modeling. He was in a medical pamphlet for an affliction known as "unusually small ears."

This is that great two-for-one joke we talked about earlier. I managed to compliment the bride AND make fun of Charlie by playing off the compliment.

Rachel coaches the dance team at the college here. Those are her students who felt obligated to cheer. But that's her job: She teaches people how to dance. And, as you'll see in just a little bit, she hasn't had a chance to give Charlie a lesson yet.

After a lot of funny stuff, Rick speaks from the heart here, and it's really nice. Sure, it can seem corny, but the bride and groom, as well as everyone else there, will love it. Trust us!

All joking aside, Charlie, you're one of my absolute best friends. From working at Mary's Italian Restaurant to soccer camp three summers in a row to that disastrous backpacking trip in Europe . . . we've been through a lot together. And I couldn't be happier for you today. I love you, buddy.

Rachel, I've gotten to know you well these past few years, and I think you're an incredible woman. As someone who knows Charlie better than anyone, I can honestly say that you two are a perfect fit for each other.

Please raise your glasses. Charlie and Rachel, congratulations. I wish you a long and happy life together.

And Rachel, please do me a favor and repeat everything I said to Charlie. He can't hear me because of his unusually small ears.

After a nice wrap-up and toast, it never hurts to add another joke! This is called a callback . . . as in "calling back" to a previous joke. This is great because all you're doing is mentioning a previous joke, but you're getting a whole new set of laughs.

Raw Elements for a Friend's Speech to Give at Her Daughter's Wedding

Carol was asked by her friend Betsy to help write a speech for her daughter Jessica's wedding. Since Carol had never met Jessica, she asked Betsy to tell her a lot about Jessica so she could help put together her speech.

Remember our earlier advice about asking other people for stories? Here are the elements Betsy gave her:

- Jessica is obsessed with classic Disney movies.

- As a little girl, she preferred playing with snails from the family garden to playing with dolls.

- Before going to preschool every morning, she wanted to put on her party dress and lipstick.

- She can be shy.

- As a little girl, she hid under the dining room table before her piano recital.

- In middle school, she was in an all-girl rock band called Go Girl.

- In college, she was a pole vaulter. Pole-vaulted with her hair down.

- As a girl, she went to a birthday party where a guy was making balloon animals. Jessica let everyone go in front of her and never got a balloon animal.

- She met her husband at A16, a camping store in West Los Angeles (which is no longer in business). She told her mom one time, "There's this guy at work who's really cute, and he kinda stares at me, so I'm pretty sure he likes me too."

AI Takes a Turn

Have you thought about AI writing your speech for you? Of course you have. Well, maybe think again. We gave AI these same raw elements, and here's what it came up with.

Ladies and gentlemen, distinguished guests,

As we gather here today to celebrate the union of two souls, I must say, it's a relief to see Jessica finally settling down. For years, her life has been like a Disney movie on fast-forward, with more twists and turns than Space Mountain!

Now let me tell you a bit about the bride. Jessica's love for Disney movies is legendary. I swear, she knows every line from *The Lion King* better than she knows her own phone number. And her commitment to classic Disney fashion? Well, let's just say she wore that princess dress before it was cool!

But Jessica's childhood wasn't just about singing woodland creatures and glass slippers. Oh no, this girl had a wild side. While other kids were playing with dolls, Jessica was out in the garden having tea parties with snails. I tell you, she had more gastropod friends than human ones!

Now let's talk about Jessica's early attempts at stardom. She may have been shy, but that didn't stop her from joining an all-girl rock band in middle school called Go Girl. And let me tell you, their rendition of "Twist and Shout" could shatter glass . . . and eardrums!

And who could forget Jessica's college years? Pole-vaulting with her hair down? That's like trying to run a marathon in glass slippers! But, hey, if anyone could pull it off, it's Jessica. She's always been one to defy expectations and embrace new challenges with style.

Of course, no speech about Jessica would be complete without mentioning her romantic escapades. I mean, who else would meet their future husband at a camping store? It's like something straight out of a rom-com, with bear repellent instead of roses!

So here we are, gathered to witness the next chapter in Jessica's adventure. And while there are no singing animals or fairy godmothers present, I have no doubt that Jessica and her husband will write a love story that's even more magical than anything Disney could dream up.

So let's raise a glass to the bride and groom as they embark on this crazy, wonderful journey called marriage. May your love be as enduring as a Disney classic, and may your adventures together be filled with laughter, joy, and maybe just a hint of fairy dust.

Cheers to the newlyweds!

There are tons of problems with this AI speech. Specifically, AI added a bunch of details to the info we fed it that are just plain *wrong*.

Jessica knows every line from *The Lion King*? Nope.

Her band played "Twist and Shout"? Didn't happen.

And even its jokes fell flat: "She had more gastropod friends than human ones"? Nothing is funny with the word *gastropod* in it. We ain't laughing and guarantee none of the guests would be either.

And what mother of the bride addresses the group as "distinguished guests"?! She's not speaking at a Rotary Club meeting.

Artificial intelligence is missing the biggest thing we keep yammering on about in this book: *a personal relationship with the person you're celebrating*. It becomes obvious within two seconds and makes it virtually (pardon the pun) impossible to compose a warm and meaningful speech.

Stay in your lane, AI! Stick to writing thank-you notes to a boss for a basket of chocolate-covered almonds, despite them forgetting you have a nut allergy.

Betsy's Real Speech for Jessica and Zack

Now let's look at the non-AI, real-human speech that Carol helped with for Betsy. Hopefully you can see that even though Carol doesn't personally know the bride, sitting down and having a conversation with her mom made a huge difference. Whether you're helping someone write a speech or writing your own, pinpoint the areas the speech-giver wants to touch on: observations, recollections, amusing stories.

AI is not interested in sitting down with anybody. Mostly because it has no legs.

I wrote her an intro with all the necessary information . . . a greeting, her name, and her relation to the bride.

Hi. I'm Betsy Goodkin, proud mother of our bride, Jessica. My husband, Dan, and I welcome you and are so happy you all came from near and far to join us for this incredible occasion. What a joy this is today to watch my beautiful daughter, my firstborn, walk down the aisle. My Disney princess who found her fairy-tale prince.

Jessica loves Disney movies, so I thought this was a sweet way to work that into the occasion.

Let me tell you a little bit about my girl because, well, we go way back. Jessica is a bit of a conundrum, in the most lovely way, of course. Like, as a little girl, she didn't love playing with dolls; she preferred playing with snails from our garden. You laugh, but trust me, I saved a ton on Barbies. And yet, before preschool, I'd wake up every morning and there she was at my bedside, saying she needed to wear her party dress and lipstick before heading over to school. She always had a sense of style, even if it was to show off to the other four-year-olds.

Real-life stories are the gold of speeches! I used this one given to me and then followed it with a joke.

→ Another example of a true and funny story, followed by a joke.

I thought this might make a good theme for the speech, since Jess has so many qualities that are the opposite of each other.

A conundrum . . . like, Jessica has an endearingly shy side, but at other times, the complete 180 of that. For example, as a little girl, she hid under the dining room table before her piano recital. But yet, in middle school, she was in an all-girl rock band called Go Girl, and they even performed at clubs a few times. I mean, when Jess takes the spotlight, she grabs it. In college, for God's sake, she pole-vaulted! And with her hair down and flowing, shunning a ponytail to stand apart! I was just happy she didn't ask for the party dress *then*!

This was a fun connection to make. How funny that the girl who hid so she didn't have to go to her piano recital ended up in a rock band that played in clubs.

Another true and funny story but this time the joke that follows is also a callback to the party dress from earlier.

Jessica always thinks of others before herself. She's incredibly generous. As a little girl, she went to a birthday party, and there was a guy making balloon animals for the kids. Jessica let everyone go in front of her, one by one, until they said he was done and it was time to cut the cake, leaving her balloon-animal-less. Well, Jess, I may be twenty-five years too late, but you do like doggies, don't you?

It's nice to work in compliments about the bride and/or groom. Especially when it's a parent giving the speech!

[*Betsy gives Jessica the balloon animal she made herself.*]

Remember, not all jokes have to be verbal. This was a good opportunity to do a physical joke, which also happens to be a sweet moment. Giving Jess the balloon animal got a big "Awwww!" But . . .

Sorry, Carol . . . I hope this doesn't ruin our friendship, but I think you missed a big opportunity here. Betsy could've given Jessica a balloon snail instead of a doggie.

But no one knows the beautiful conundrum that is our daughter like her partner in crime, Zack. I love the story of how you two met. They met six years ago working at A16, the camping store in West LA. She came home one night and said, "There's this guy at work who's really cute, and he kinda stares at me, so I'm pretty sure he likes me too." How great is that? Zack, you set our daughter's heart aflutter in a *camping store*? That's bragging rights, my new

It's also important to mention the groom and the fun story of how they met. Everyone loves to know what brought the two together.

son-in-law. Yeti cups and half-dome tents are not what we typically think of as aphrodisiacs!

The more specific you can get with your jokes, the funnier they will be. Saying "cups" and "tents" doesn't paint quite as detailed a picture as "Yeti cups" and "half-dome tents."

Yiddish for "meant to be"

Thought it would be nice to bring back around Jessica's love of Disney movies at the end. Puts a nice cap on the speech!

Jessica and Zack, Dan and I wish you nothing but the best and buckets of love from this day forward. A16 might have gone out of business, but you two came out afloat; it was definitely bashert. And since I know you share a love of Disney movies, I will end with a quote from Snow White, the classic Disney character, who said, "I'm wishing for the one I love to find me today." Well, mission accomplished. Please join me now in raising our glasses to Jessica and Zack and wishing them a hearty mazel tov!

Because it was a Jewish ceremony, "mazel tov" was included. Always end by raising a glass and saying a heartfelt congratulations in whatever way!

Cousin Elliot's Best Man Speech for His Brother Joel

Carol's relative gave this speech at his youngest brother's wedding, and it's such a knockout! Even more so because Elliot, the speech-giver, is on the quiet side in real life. He wrote and performed this speech like such a champ, getting loads of laughs. It's posted on YouTube and has so many hits because it's just the perfect package of funny and warm. Check this out!

Good evening. My name is Elliot Levitt, and I am Joel's oldest brother. I have to be honest, I actually had a hard time thinking of good Joel stories that I could tell tonight. I talked to my brother Max a couple of weeks ago; he had good stories, but he was using them in his own speech. And I talked to my parents the other day, and they had a lot of stories, but none that I felt really captured the essence of who Joel is. In a moment of total desperation, I actually tried calling Cooper, Joel and Jill's dog, to see if he had any ideas, but I never got past his secretary.

It's never a bad idea to open by stating a universal fear of speech-giving. Admitting this vulnerability gets the guests on your side right off the bat.

First joke out of the box. Lets people know this is going to be a funny speech.

I think to understand why it's so hard to think of good Joel stories, you kinda have to know what the dynamic was of the Levitt brothers when we were kids. I, as the eldest, was usually off in a corner somewhere with my head in a book. I was very quiet, very independent. And this was probably for the best because, as the middle child, Max needed a lot of attention—throwing temper tantrums, running into walls, stepping on rusty nails in third-world countries, this was Max. And you really couldn't take your eyes off him for a second.

As for Joel, I think I first met Joel when I was, like, twelve. I said to my parents one day, "Why is there this other room attached to Max's bathroom?" And they said, "That belongs to your younger brother." I asked, "Max?" And they said, "No, no, there's another one. He's even younger than Max. His name is Joel." I went in, and, sure enough, there he was, sitting in a hammock picking his nose.

I introduced myself. He seemed to know who I was, he was very polite, we exchanged pleasantries and went our separate ways. As the years went on, I'd run into Joel from time to time. On a family trip, I might turn to look in the back of the rental van, and there he'd be, gazing quietly out the window, picking his nose. I'd wave and he'd smile back, and I might not see him again for several months.

Time went by; I went to college, I moved away, but my parents would give me updates on Joel from time to time. At one point, they told me he'd started working as a volunteer firefighter, which sounded really impressive until one day they called and said I should watch the news that night. There was a big house fire in Bethesda. Joel's station was called, he texted them in the afternoon, and we'd actually be able to see him on the news story about the fire. So I tuned in that night, excited to see Joel in action, and sure enough there was this house with flames pouring out of the doors and windows. Firefighters were rushing in with hoses and axes, and they're running out with babies and puppies. And in the middle of it all is Joel, clad head to toe in his firefighting gear, holding his phone, texting my parents to let them know that he'd be on TV that night.

Where was I going from there? . . .

Continuing his funny theme of barely knowing his brother.

Second mention of the runner.

GREAT use of a personal family story that pokes fun at Joel.

It's totally fine to share with the audience that you've lost your train of thought. Give yourself a break— you're not in a staged production of Les Mis, for God's sake!

At one point, on what I had actually thought was just a routine family trip to Bloomington, Indiana, I actually found myself at Joel's college graduation. I hadn't even known he was *in* college at the time. And as I looked down on him sitting among his fellow graduates, holding his diploma, picking his nose, I couldn't help but feel a certain twinge of pride.

Elliot continuing the funny through line of not knowing his brother.

The third and last appearance of the nose-picking runner!

What followed was a somewhat prolonged job search during which Joel learned that when filling out your application to join the police academy, it's best not to mention the night you spent in jail under "Experience." That's a story probably best reserved for another occasion, but suffice to say that, much like asking his older brothers to roast him at his own wedding, it was a mistake Joel won't be making again.

Another personal story, capped off by a funny joke.

There was no need to worry. Joel did eventually manage to land a really great position at the Nellis Corporation [a family business], following what I'm sure was a highly competitive interview process in which he promised to finally move out of our parents' house in exchange for a weekly salary.

The perfect joke for a kid who works in the family business!

Before long, it came to my attention that Joel had begun seeing a young woman named Jill, and that this Jill had actually moved in with Joel and Max in their house in Washington, DC.

Although instead of paying rent or her share of the utilities, she would just buy Joel a pair of sunglasses every once in a while, an arrangement that I'm sure Joel genuinely believed made financial sense.

Not only a funny personal story, but it also incorporates and pokes a little fun at the bride.

Following a few years of blissful cohabitation, one unfortunate incident occurred in which Jill walked in on Max while he was taking a shower, so it was then decided that it might be best if Joel and Jill just struck off on their own.

Perfect example of why personal stories are always a hit in speeches. Who knew that was the reason the couple moved out on their own?!

Joel and Jill moved in together, and before long, I received an ecstatic call from my mother telling me that Jill had begun the process of converting to Judaism. I was kind of baffled as to why anyone would want to do such a thing until I learned that, despite his love of pork and blonds and paying retail, Joel is actually Jewish himself.

Not only a funny joke but still working the theme of not knowing his brother very well!

Through all of this, and as proud as I was of Joel and his many accomplishments, there was this feeling that I just couldn't really shake, which is that I wasn't really sure what his point was. Like I just wasn't really sure why he was there. You know, my parents already had one perfectly good child, and Max, and having a third just seemed kind of superfluous.

This is a feeling that actually nagged at me for decades until finally, just a few years ago, the whole family was together. We were talking about having kids for some reason, and I said that I would want to have probably no more than two myself, and my mother immediately jumped in and said, "No, no, Elliot, you have to have three like I did because what if something happens to one of the first two?" Some of you, I sense, are coming to the same realization that I had in this moment, which is that Joel was always just the "insurance child," in case I got hit by a truck or Max drank a bottle of Windex or something, the latter of which is admittedly still plausible.

So I thought maybe I would take this opportunity, while we're all here and Joel's surrounded by his family and friends, to just say, "Joel, thank you for your service." I know thirty years is a really long time to be on standby, ready to jump in and assume the role of a real person at any moment. So I just want to congratulate you as you now move on to your new role as Jill's insurance husband. Someone for her to fall back on in case she doesn't run into Oscar Isaac in a bar in the next few years. But until that day, I just want to say mazel tov, and let's hear it once more for Joel, the insurance child!

This is a great example of taking a real-life "family moment" and expounding on it for comedic effect. That Elliot explains it as Joel being "the insurance child" in the family was super clever and creative.

A sweet ending that puts a cap on everything. Even if it's funny, always end on something heartfelt. It's a big deal to toast your brother at his wedding; wrap it up sincerely!

Rick's Speech for Ella and Jake's Wedding

Let's take a look at Rick's wedding speech for Ella and Jake. Pay attention to how Rick really loads on the comedy so well in this speech. But at the end, he speaks from the heart. It's so important to add some warmth when you close.

Starting out funny! Always gets people's attention.

My name is Rick. For those of you who don't know me . . . that's really too bad for you. Because I'm a wonderful person. I'm adorable to boot. And I have an incredible body. But we're not here just to talk about me.

We're here to talk about the wedding of these two people . . . Bella and Blake. I'm sorry . . . Ella and Jake. Okay, whatever. It doesn't matter. Names are irrelevant. You know who I'm talking about.

Messing up the bride's and groom's names. If it worked before, it'll work again!

I met Ella our freshman year at UC Davis. In our dorm, our rooms actually shared a wall. One night, I was trying to sleep, but the music coming from her room was so loud. So I knocked on Ella's door and asked if she could turn it down. But while I was standing there at her door, I could hear that the music wasn't really all that loud; it was just the bass that was bothering me. But Ella was super nice— she said sure and lowered the volume.

I saw Ella the next day and ended up apologizing to her. She thought it was funny, the thing about the bass, and we became friends after that.

Sorry, Rick, I know it's too late to change this because you already gave this speech, but I think this story of how you met could be structured a little better. It might make more sense to go from asking Ella to turn it down, to her saying sure, to then saying . . .

When I got back to my room, I realized the music hadn't really been all that loud. It was just the bass that was bothering me. I saw Ella the next day and ended up apologizing to her. She thought it was funny, the bass thing, and we became friends after that.

There's a callback to the bass at the end of the speech, so this is a better joke placement.

At UC Davis, Ella majored in English. Now she's in the midst of pursuing a master's degree in English. There's even talk of her pursuing a PhD in English. I mean, look, Ella, if you don't know the language by now . . .

As for her recent husband, Jake, he's a high school biology teacher. A lot of people always thought Ella would marry into money. And the fact is, she did marry into money. It's just very little money. Very, very little money.

It was a beautiful service, don't you think? There was that one point where the priest said, "If anyone feels there's a reason that these two should not be wed, speak now or forever hold your peace." And, of course, no one said anything, because I got there late. I should be with Ella. It could've worked out. It could've. As long as I didn't take her last name. Then I would be Rick Shaw.

Keep drinking. This'll go a lot easier for you guys.

It doesn't seem that long ago when Ella said to me, "Rick, I just met this amazing guy. He's sweet. He takes great care of me. And he's just absolutely gorgeous." And I was like, does Jake know about this guy? You should tell him. And if you don't, I'll tell everyone at the wedding reception.

Lovely sentiment at the end here.

Now I should get serious. This'll be awkward. Ella, I'm honored that you would include me in your wedding and let me speak. It's truly a pleasure. I'm so happy to see that you've found someone. Jake, I don't really know you all that well, but it doesn't matter. Because Ella is such a wonderful person, I know that anyone she would choose to marry would be equally as wonderful. Best of luck to the both of you. And if the wedding DJ's bass is too loud, you won't hear a word from me. To the bride and groom!

Great callback to "the bass" and his "how I met Ella" story!

Carol's Speech at Cousin Jay's Memorial

So now that you have the hang of a wedding speech and can give one no problem (right?), you may be wondering, "Well, what am I supposed to do if the event isn't a wedding? What if it's even a serious, somber event, like someone has passed away? What do I do *then*?" No worries; we got you covered.

Let's have a look at the speech Carol wrote for her cousin Jay's memorial. It's important to remember at these events the gravity of the situation. Someone loved by many has lost their life, so a sense of decorum should always be present in the speech. However, it's okay to add in some humor. People appreciate a light touch at a memorial to break the solemnity of the event and to remind everyone of the joy this person brought.

Take note of how well Carol balanced paying sincere tribute to Jay with being funny.

Good afternoon and thank you all for coming to honor the passing of Jay Levitt. Fifty-eight years. For someone who lived so large, cancer robbed him big-time. Jay is technically my wife, Lori's, first cousin. But the nice thing about being with someone for over twenty-six years is that those "official" bloodlines start to blur, winding up at "Are they your relative or mine? I've completely forgotten." So I will always think of Jay as my full cousin too.

It's so bizarre that Jay's not here with us today, right? Because Jay was such a social person. He *lived* to be around other people. So I picture him wherever he is now, looking around and saying, "What's everybody doing? Why didn't you *call me*?"

I'm proud to tell you that I was the one who officially dubbed Jay "The Pied Piper of Fun." Because every day spent with Jay was an adventure. He picked up that magic flute, and we all followed merrily behind him.

A really nice and fun way to compliment Jay. He was obviously the life of the party, and everyone there will enjoy remembering him that way.

This paragraph is a very nice story about Jay's generosity and authenticity. Sometimes it's hard for people to put their finger on what they loved so much about someone. They appreciate when a speaker can put it into words.

As we all know, Jay and Jeni had their boat, the *Mikoh*. And they were kind enough to invite us, and many of us here, to join them on these incredible trips—to Cabo, Puerto Vallarta, and La Paz, Mexico. And the beauty of those trips was we spent an enormous amount of real time together. Literally, breakfast to beddy-bye time. And that time was rich. A lot of laughs, goofing around, but kinda deep here and there because that's what real time brings. That everyday life we find ourselves in—texting, emailing, head down in each of our devices—who even talks on the phone anymore? That was the gold of Jay: his approach to life, which was all about spending quality time, eyeball to eyeball, with family and friends. He lived for it. And this was always the case, even before he got ill.

Humorously pointing out the technology routine we've all fallen into makes everyone appreciate how special their time was with Jay.

Joie de vivre. It's the best way I could encapsulate his attitude toward life. I mean, that big belly laugh of his! How could any of us here today forget it?

People don't need to fall out of their seats laughing at a memorial service. It can be enough just mentioning qualities everyone loves about the person.

Don't get me wrong, no one worked harder than Jay. Everyone here recognizes that tableau—Jay on the boat at the breakfast table, laptop in front of him, in the *zone*. Getting some serious shit done. Always.

I don't think I would've risked dropping an "sh-bomb" at a memorial service. Carol is much braver than I am. But Carol's years of experience as a stand-up comic mean she knows how to read a room very, very well. You, on the other hand, probably don't. So don't risk it, and keep it clean.

Another great quality about Jay and a nice self-reflection from Carol. She's not just talking about Jay's passing; she's deriving meaning from it, which people appreciate in light of losing a loved one.

But still, he devoted a hefty part of his life to *fun*. His passing has really made me think about that a lot. Fun. It gets short shrift in life. It feels frivolous, secondary in some way to everything else "important." And yet, what will stand out at the front of the line to each of us when it's all over? Ten to one, it's gonna be the fun. And Jay knew that a long, long time ago.

Another thing I found remarkable about Jay? For someone in recovery, he partied harder than anyone I know without drugs or alcohol. He really figured that one out.

I want to note that I asked Jay's wife beforehand if it was okay to make this joke. She loved it. Had she not liked it, I would, of course, have taken it out.

Music? Did anyone love music more than Jay? Aimee? [Aimee Mann and her band played at Jay's memorial.] I guarantee Jay knows you're here today, and he's freaking out!

Harry Styles, Pink, Red Hot Chili Peppers, the Rolling Stones. Lemme ask you something: Did Jay make you watch Talking Heads' *Stop Making Sense* movie as many times as he made us?

Jay really was the ultimate people person. The last time Lori and I saw Jay and Jeni, we went to see the Beach Boys at the Greek Theatre in Los Angeles. I had a connection, so we were invited to the private party with the band after the show. I was nervous because I was dying to go over to Mike Love, one of the original Beach

Great story. Even if you don't know Jay, it makes you appreciate how carefree and fun he was.

Boys, and say hello. See, I had opened for the band back in 1982 at Harrah's in Lake Tahoe, and I wanted to see if he would remember me. So I'm pacing in a corner by myself at the party, trying to figure out how I'm gonna go up to Mike Love, seamlessly, without making a jerk of myself. So I finally gather the courage, I look over to where Mike Love is now in the room, and what do I see? Jay and Mike Love, talking and laughing it up, looking like the oldest of dear friends. I walk over, and Jay says, "Mike! Do you happen to remember my cousin Carol from a gig she did with you back in the day?" Classic Jay.

I really like this paragraph because it's not just remembering how great Jay was, but challenging everyone there to live life the way he did.

So, everybody? Let's take a little lesson from our beloved Jay and get off our phones and actually see, talk, and be with each other way more. The way Jay did it too. Face to face—the bliss of a real, good conversation, the ebb and flow back and forth. And let's never forget fun! Yeah, fun.

Jay? In my heart, you are not really gone, only relocated. Because I know somewhere up there, you've picked up that magic flute, and, to no one's surprise, a band of angels is already following joyfully behind you.

A "callback" to the beginning of the speech where I affectionately referred to Jay as "The Pied Piper of Fun." Thought it'd be satisfying to bring it back around as a button to the speech.

The
End

Wrapping It Up

Well, you've finally arrived at the end of your speech! We know that because your heart is no longer racing and your palms have returned to their normal unclammy state. We hope you feel a real sense of accomplishment, because this wrapping-it-up part is a breeze compared with the laughfest you worked so hard on delivering earlier. Why a breeze? Because there's no pressure to be funny anymore. Time to speak from the heart for a moment. Sincerity . . . it's the best bow you can wrap around your speech.

As an easy segue in, you can say something as simple as this: "But let me get serious for a moment. . . ." And then get serious for a moment.

Now, we're not saying you need to pull out the Kleenex and tell your friend that he "completes you" or burst into your rendition of Adele's "Make You Feel My Love," but say something nice. Even if you're a person who never gets serious, use this special day as an opportunity to tell the bride and groom or whomever something sweet that you might not normally say. There's a reason they asked you to give a speech. It's a high honor in the Book of Relationships and says a lot about your importance in their lives. So show them some love back.

"What would life be without their friendship over the years?"

"It was sometimes a bumpy road to graduation, but you crushed it!"

"A lot of hard work and grit went into this retirement. It was truly earned."

"No more Hebrew tutor, kid! How 'bout that?"

"'The one' was always out there. You just had to find her."

It doesn't matter what you say, as long as it's real and honest. Trust us, they will appreciate it. And guaranteed, all the guests will too. (Even the ones who could have lived without "your little jokes.")

A piece of advice is always a nice feature. Say you're someone who's been married for a long time; the couple knows you speak from experience: "Never go to bed angry. Stay up and duke it out until you win."

Or: "Remember, marriage is a marathon, not a sprint. And just like a marathon, sometimes your nipples will get chafed." Maybe at a graduation: "The world is your oyster. Unfortunately, with those student loans, you can't afford oysters." So feel free at any occasion to add something funny from your personal experience. The personal is always the best go-to in any speech.

And definitely don't forget this! At the end of your speech, raise your glass and toast the honoree(s)! We then recommend going over to give them a warm embrace. Puts a nice cap on it all. (It's so weird when someone gives an amazing toast and then just abruptly, awkwardly, heads back to their seat.)

Now you are officially certified to go get hammered at the (hopefully) open bar. Don't you just hate a cash bar at these things?

Way to go, speech-giver!

THE END TIPS

To recap:

- [ ] **Speak from the heart briefly.**
- [ ] **Raise a glass and toast your honoree(s).**
- [ ] **Give them a warm embrace before going back to your seat.**

Public-Speaking Tips & Tricks

Right off the bat, give yourself a break. You don't give speeches for a living, and the audience is rooting for you! When we perform at comedy clubs, people expect us to be funny. Very funny. And rightfully so. The audience paid to laugh. But when a guest gets up to give a speech at an event, the bar is set to non-pro low. No one's expecting you to be Jerry Seinfeld up there. Not everyone is hysterical, especially your dad. So tell him to stop making those horrible dad jokes.

A few days before the event, start practicing your speech. Try it out on a few people—ideally people who know whomever you're toasting. But if they don't, just try to practice it in front of folks you trust enough to give you honest feedback. And when you get tired of the honest feedback, try it out in front of your dog. Rex delights in everything you do.

"Can I read my speech?"

Of course. But remember, you're not delivering "Still I Rise" by Maya Angelou. Make sure you go slowly, pick your head up to look at the audience here and there, and connect with them. You worked so hard to put this amazing speech together; for God's sake, have fun with it!

If you can, instead of reading, it's always better to have bullet points written on an index card. This keeps the flow of your speech more natural. But if the idea of a card still makes you tense, by all means, go ahead and read your speech.

"But I'm nervous!"

Of course you're nervous! Do you know how many shows we've done over the years? And we still get nervous. It's part of the process. But what will help immensely is finding out the details before the event. When will you be speaking? Are all the speakers talking one after another? Or will the speeches be separated? Where will you be standing? At your table? In the center of the room? Will you have a microphone? The more you can find out, the better you'll be.

"What do I do if I forget part of my speech?"

Don't be afraid to just be yourself. "I just blanked here, guys, brain fart, gimme a second." People will appreciate your honesty and spontaneity.

"What do I do if nobody is laughing?"

Well, that question is 101 for any comedian, and Carol will share some advice she got from the great comic Richard Belzer when she asked that exact same thing when she was starting out: "You are the pilot of the audience. If you seem like the reaction to you is A-OK and everything is hunky-dory, they will too." You have no idea how many shows we thought we were bombing until a parade of people came over afterward, saying, "You were *great!*"

"What if I'm so nervous that I want to bail?"

Now, here's where speeches can careen off a cliff if you're not careful. DON'T DRINK TOO MUCH BEFORE YOU SPEAK. (We haven't used all caps the entire book until now, so that should show you how serious we are.) Speakers want to relax, so they have a cocktail. Absolutely normal. But as the time they're supposed to get up there draws nearer and nearer, one cocktail becomes three, or eight. Don't sabotage yourself by unwittingly getting wasted. Treat your toast as work. Get the job done, and then you can get as drunk as you want, providing you are over twenty-one. Or perhaps younger, if you live outside of the United States.

And don't use hard drugs like heroin or crack cocaine. This isn't just for the speech; we recommend always staying away from these narcotics. We care and we've grown very fond of you!

Templates

Who doesn't love
a cheat sheet?

If you're feeling
stuck, here are
fill-in-the-blanks
templates for a variety
of occasions. A handy
GPS to follow.

Wedding-Speech Template

Feeling lost? Try this wedding-speech template.

Hello, my name is _____, and
YOUR NAME

I'm _____. I remember when I first
RELATIONSHIP TO HONOREE (X)

met _____, _____
X

_____.
WHERE AND WHEN YOU MET X

If you're related, no need for this. Unless you grew up in a very dysfunctional household.

Now, everybody knows that _____
X

is _____. And I
A CHARACTERISTIC OR QUALITY OF X

saw this very clearly when _____
X

_____
SOMETHING X DID TO DISPLAY THIS CHARACTERISTIC OR QUALITY

_____

_____

_____.

_____? You're lucky because

_____ is a very good person.

_____ once _____

_____

_____

_____.

But of course, I've also got to tell you the funniest story

about _____. _____

_____

_____

_____

_____.

*When we suggest "embarrassing,"
we mean "he once actually slipped
on a banana peel" embarrassing.
Not "he once came into work
drunk, lost his job, his house,
and his first wife" embarrassing.

And then _____ met _____.
X · Y

I'll never forget when _____ told me.
X

_____

_____

_____

_____.

Now, it's plain to see that _____ is
Y

_____.

And it's clear to see these two should be together because

_____.

_____ was a disaster as a single person!
X

_____ once _____
X

_____

_____

_____

_____.

Today, we toast their marriage! _____?

Y

You're going to have to get used to a lot of things about

_____.

X

_____

THREE FUNNY THINGS ABOUT X THAT YOU ARE SURE WILL DRIVE Y CRAZY

_____

_____

_____.

So let's raise our glasses to _____ and

X

_____. I am honored that you asked

Y

me to speak on this monumental occasion and wish you

nothing but the best from this day forward! Cheers!

Things Not to Say in Your Wedding Speech!

- I recognize one of the groomsmen from *America's Most Wanted*.

- She's an eleven. He's barely a five.

- *One* bartender?

- Maybe this is the gummies talking . . .

- It's nice to see he married outside the family this time.

- That flower girl sucked.

- You can tell both moms had a little nip and tuck prewedding.

- I recognize his dad from his profile pic on Tinder.

- Who wants the over on five years, not me.

Things Not to Say to the Bride

- Finally!

- You look just like his mother.

- It's a shame you didn't get your first choice of venue.

- That should clear up in about a week.

- Did you think about this enough?

- I'm sure you'll get it right the next time.

- You're carrying so well!

- Trying a completely new hairstyle on your wedding day, that is bold!

- I know white is the appropriate color for a wedding dress, but black is always slimming.

- Watch your back; his nana is not to be trusted.

- His family members seem like drinkers.

- Has he talked to you about a threesome yet? He will. And I'm in.

Jokes to Steal—"Didn't Want to Spend a Lot of Money on the Wedding"

- He tried to propose with a Ring Pop.

- They passed on the Elvis impersonator, finding him "costly."

- Their idea of an open bar is a bar down the street that's open.

- The bride is tossing a handful of seeds instead of a bouquet.

- The parking valet is the groom's brother Cooper, who needs the practice for driver's ed.

- The food they're serving came in the cans tied to the car the newlyweds are leaving in.

- The wedding band is a tribute band to a Queen tribute band.

- The venue needs to be empty by nine p.m. for an AA meeting.

Things Not to Say at Someone's Third or Fourth Wedding

- Tonight, try to remember to scream out the right name.

- The color white called, claiming fraud.

- She invited one of the bridesmaids from her first wedding, but she's in an assisted-living facility in Boca Raton now.

- The wedding planner asked, "The usual?"

- If history is any indication, I hope you all kept your receipts for the wedding gifts.

- I'm calling it now. In six months, he's the next Golden Bachelor.

- The florist's business is entirely just the bride's weddings now.

- He's tied the knot so many times, he's now an honorary Boy Scout.

- At this point, she might as well catch her own bouquet.

- His weddings are like the Olympics—there's one every four years.

- You know what they say: "Never a bridesmaid, always a bride."

Retirement-Speech Template

Feeling lost? Try this retirement-speech template.

Hello, my name is _____, and
YOUR NAME

I'm _____. I remember when I first
RELATIONSHIP TO RETIREE (X)

started working with _____,
X

_____.
WHERE AND WHEN YOU MET X

↰ *If you're related,
no need for this.*

_____ has had quite a career.
X

In their _____ working at
LENGTH OF TIME

_____,
NAME OF COMPANY

_____ accomplished so much.
X

_____
LIST SOME OF X'S BIGGEST ACCOMPLISHMENTS

_____

_____

_____.

Of course, I'm not surprised by any of this, because _____

_____
A CHARACTERISTIC OR QUALITY OF X

_____. I remember one time

_____
SOMETHING X DID TO DISPLAY THIS CHARACTERISTIC OR QUALITY

_____

_____.

Yes, at times I wondered if _____ might get
X

fired. Let me tell you this story about _____.
X

_____
A FUNNY OR EMBARRASSING STORY ABOUT X

_____

_____

_____

_____.

It's hard to imagine _____ not being at
X

_____.
NAME OF COMPANY

Now that _____ will have more time,
X

they say they're going to _____
X'S PLANS

_____.

I think that's a _____ because
"GOOD IDEA"/"BAD IDEA"

_____
FUNNY REASON WHY YOU THINK X'S PLAN IS A GOOD IDEA OR A BAD IDEA

_____

_____

_____.

But I'll tell you what I'll miss most about _____.
X

_____
WHAT YOU'LL MISS MOST ABOUT X

_____. Let me tell you why.

_____
FUNNY STORY ABOUT WHY YOU'LL MISS THAT THING ABOUT X

_____

_____

_____

_____.

So let's raise our glasses to _____!
X

Thank you for your years of hard work. I wish you all the

best in retirement. This is it, even if you want to come back!

Congratulations on an amazing career and a well-deserved

break. Now go relax! Cheers!

Jokes to Steal—"It's Time to Retire"

- She was old three hips ago.

- She went apple picking with Eve.

- Her version of a Caesar salad was actually sharing a salad with Julius Caesar.

- Her birthday-cake candles were nixed. The EPA shut them down on account of global warming.

- She still calls movies "talkies."

- Moses was her personal accountant.

- When she married her first husband, she said, "I doeth."

- Her first honeymoon was in Pangaea.

- She had a pet *T. rex* named Mr. Chompers.

- She opened for Fire and the Wheel.

Graduation-Speech Template

Feeling lost? Try this graduation-speech template.

Hello, my name is _____, and

I'm _____. I remember when I first

met _____, _____

_____.

← If you're related, no need for this.

I'm so proud that _____ is graduating.

I always knew _____ would because

of _____

_____. I remember one time

_____

_____

_____

_____.

Of course, at times I had my doubts _____
_X

would make it to the finish line. Let me tell you this story

about _____. _____
_X

_____
A FUNNY OR EMBARRASSING STORY ABOUT X

_____

_____

_____.

As you know, _____ majored in
_X

_____.
X'S MAJOR

*If high school graduation,
mention their strongest subject.*

Looking back, this makes a lot of sense. _____

_____
A FUNNY OR EMBARRASSING STORY THAT SHOWS

_____
WHY THAT MAJOR OR SUBJECT IS PERFECT FOR X

_____

_____.

_____ was also very active in
X

_____.
A SPORT OR ACTIVITY X TOOK PART IN

I have to tell you this story. _____

_____
A FUNNY OR EMBARRASSING STORY ABOUT X'S SPORT OR ACTIVITY

_____

_____

_____.

Now that _____ has graduated, next
X

_____ is going to _____
X   X'S PLANS

_____

_____

_____.

Mention whether X has a job,
is going to do more school,
will be traveling, or plans
to do nothing.

I think that's a _____,

"GOOD IDEA"/"BAD IDEA"

and I'll tell you why. _____

_____

FUNNY REASON WHY YOU THINK X'S PLAN IS A GOOD IDEA OR A BAD IDEA

_____

_____

_____.

So let's raise our glasses to _____!

X

I wish you all the best in the future. I know you'll be

successful at whatever you do. Congratulations and cheers!

Bar Mitzvah–Speech Template

Usually a parent gives the speech. Feeling the pressure
of not knowing what to say to your child on this
momentous day? Take a spin with this road map.

Bar mitzvah—boy
Bat mitzvah—girl

Good evening. My name is _____
YOUR NAME

and I'm _____.
RELATIONSHIP TO HONOREE (X)

What a momentous and memorable day this is for you,

as you become a bar mitzvah. And for all of us here to

share, having had the joy of watching you grow. It seems

like only yesterday when _____

_____
A FUNNY OR ENDEARING MEMORY OF X AS A CHILD

_____
OR A STORY ABOUT THE ORIGIN OF THEIR HEBREW NAME

_____

_____

_____.

Getting to this day is quite an achievement. It takes a lot

of hard work and dedication, but you did it! You read your

Torah and haftarah portions beautifully. Your speech was

thoughtful and insightful. You did us all proud. Our family is

especially happy we got here to the finish line in one piece,

because there was that one time in the run-up to today

when _____
A FUNNY OR EMBARRASSING STORY ABOUT SOMETHING

_____
THAT HAPPENED DURING THE STUDYING PROCESS

_____

_____

_____

_____

_____.

Your bar mitzvah marks a huge accomplishment, but it's

only the beginning of everything a _____
"YOUNG MAN"/"YOUNG WOMAN"

like you is going to achieve.

This speech wouldn't be complete, of course, without a big

thank-you to _____

for all their help and guidance along the way.

_____, I'm sure you're very relieved.
          X

Tomorrow, it's finally back to _____
                                              VIDEO GAME

and _____
                    X'S FAVORITE SOCIAL MEDIA

_____.

← *(or whatever activities they love and had to take a break from)*

So let's all raise our glasses! Kids, raise your Cokes! And

join me in saying mazel tov to _____!
                                                 X

Things Not to Say to the Bar Mitzvah Boy

- Oh, those will drop soon.

- Today, you become a man. Tomorrow, it's back on the bus to seventh grade.

- Torah? The way you read, it was more like "Bore-ah."

- Is that a yad in your pocket, or are you just happy to see me?

- Don't take anything in crypto.

- Clearasil has a money-back guarantee.

- Your voice had more cracks in it than a drunk girl's iPhone.

- Can I borrow your yarmulke to cover my bald spot?

- Your mom looked hot dancing the hora.

- Guess what? There's a second bris!

Things Not to Say at a Funeral

- All right, who's ready to put the "fun" in "funeral"?

- Even in death, she sees whoever brought the flowers from the roadside stand.

- If I heard that fishing story of his one more time . . .

- I mean, he *was* in his eighties.

- I called this one. Diane, you owe me ten bucks.

- Margaret, I'm sorry for your loss. But since you're single now . . .

- Her hair and makeup never looked this good when she was alive.

- She still has a casserole dish of mine from the holidays.

We made up some speeches by some of our favorite movie and TV characters. Can you find where they did well and where they could improve? It's not a quiz or anything, we just thought it would be fun.

CARMELA SOPRANO'S SPEECH AT TONY SOPRANO'S RETIREMENT PARTY

Good evening, everyone. My name is Carmela Soprano, and I'm Tony's wife. I hope everyone found parking. And I also hope you have someone to start your car for you when you leave. Thank you for joining us on this momentous occasion, Tony Soprano's retirement! I guess age catches up with all of us. Tony's so old now that when someone tells him to "fuhgeddaboudit," he actually does.

The years we've shared together, marone! I'll never forget our first date. Tony took me to an arcade, and I could already tell he was different from any other guy I'd gone out with. When we played Whac-A-Mole, he got frustrated with just the mallet, took out his gun, and mowed all the moles down. It might've been the very first time I had to remind Tony that it wasn't personal.

And what would our life be without our kids, Meadow and A.J.? They had different childhoods, for sure. I mean, how many kids find $50K in Krugerrands and a .45 automatic on an Easter egg hunt? But that's what makes their stories at dinner parties so interesting now.

Eat up, paisans! We made it special and got the best gabagool and braciole, and the finest buffalo mozzarella from Tenuta Vannulo in Italy. Trust me, none of it fell off a truck.

I'm excited for our move down to the condo in Boca Raton. Life will be different for sure. The only agita I'll have when Tony leaves in the morning is wondering if he'll pull something playing pickleball. And the look on the property manager's face when Tony pays the HOA each month from a shoebox of cash? Priceless!

Of course, the early bird special at Olive Garden won't be anywhere near as good as the food at Artie Bucco's place back home, but, hey, look at it this way. They already have all-you-can-eat breadsticks, so no need to slip a C-note to the hostess.

Look, Tony, I know how much you'll miss the Bada Bing. How many men have their base of operations in a strip club? But I'm sure you'll find plenty of "putans" down in Florida like you did here in Jersey.

Older ones, granted. But if there's any way for you
to develop a kink for orthopedic shoes, you'll find
it. The beauty of our marriage is, no matter how
many goomars you've had over the years, you always
come home to me, cara mio.

Having you home all the time now—what a treat
that's gonna be. Maybe you can actually take out the
garbage once or twice, seeing as you had an entire
career as a "waste-management consultant."

Retirement with you, Tony, I know will be a blast.
I can't wait for the day when you push that Life Alert
button and say, "Help! I've fallen! And no one can
help me because I'm in witness protection!"

So to wrap it all up, since tonight is a really big deal,
I have a little surprise for you all. I'm wired right now.
That was a joke. Maybe.

ELAINE BENES'S WEDDING TOAST TO JERRY SEINFELD

Good evening. I'm Elaine Benes, Jerry's very dear old friend. Tonight, we say goodbye to Independent Jerry. All I have to say is, you guys getting married? Get out!

As some of you may know, Jerry and I used to date back in the day, and that's probably a story for another time. But needless to say, we did have sex thirty-seven times. And then three more after we broke up.

[*Elaine feels the chilly reaction of the room.*]

Off to a good start here!

It's a great story of how Jerry met his bride. Boy meets girl, yada yada yada, and here we are tonight.

[*Elaine turns to the bride.*]

Let's just thank the dear Lord that your first name doesn't rhyme with a female body part, like that Dolores. And as a reminder, you two, don't start calling each other "Schmoopy" either.

Well, Jerry's beautiful bride, you did the impossible. You got Seinfeld to settle down. And that's no small feat, because this was a guy with a lot of quirky turnoffs. He once broke up with a woman because she shushed him while he was watching TV. He ended it with a woman who ate her peas one at a time. And when he found a tube of fungicide in a date's medicine cabinet, he just had to get the hell outta there. So kudos to *you*!

Jerry, you asked me to be your eyes and ears around here tonight, and I've got nothing but good news to report. I personally vetted the parking valets, and they are all showered and smelling like daisies. Not one trace of BO. And I kept a keen eye out at the cocktail reception, and you'll be very glad to hear that not one of your guests "double-dipped" with the chips.

Jerry and the Mrs., they've certainly gone over the top with this wedding, don't you think? I mean, just look at these flowers. They're real, and they're spectacular!

Your ceremony was so lovely and moving too. Especially impressive because Jerry has never been one to feel the gravity of big moments like these. I mean, he was once caught making out with a date during *Schindler's List*.

And I hope everyone was careful with the wedding presents. I'll tell you right now, Jerry won't accept anything from a regifter.

Jerry did ask me to pass along that there will be a soup station as part of the dinner, so please! Keep the line moving; speak your soup in a loud, clear voice; step to the left; and receive your soup. And if there's a salad, I pray it's a big one.

I hope you both are thinking about starting a family soon. I just can't wait to hear Jerry say, "You gotta see the baay-beee!"

And a little birdie told me that they're off to Saint Croix for their honeymoon—lovely! Just be careful, Jer, after a dip in the cool ocean. You know, shrinkage and all.

But before I go, I gotta find this woman here tonight. There was no toilet paper in my stall in the ladies' room. So I asked the person in the next stall for some, and she said, "I don't have a square to spare." Can you believe *the nerve*? As God is my witness, I will track you down.

Okay, that's it for me, folks. And strike up the band because guess who'll be the first one out on the dance floor? Me!

HAN SOLO'S
BAR MITZVAH TOAST
TO CHEWBACCA

Hi, my name is Han Solo, and I'd like to say a few words about my best friend, Chewie. I can't believe it. Today, this Wookiee boy becomes a Wookiee man.

I first met Chewie years ago when I was captured by the Empire and thrown into a pit where a "beast" that hadn't been fed in a couple of days lived. That beast turned out to be a seven-foot monster named Chewbacca. He would've killed me, but luckily, I spoke a little Shyriiwook. Thank God for my Rosetta Stone language app.

But it turns out all those weird sounds Chewie made weren't his native language. He was just reciting his haftarah.

Anyway, as we were trapped in this pit, I told him we should help each other escape. And we did. So, yes, technically Chewie is a rescue.

For those of you who don't know, and I know this makes the rabbi especially proud, Chewie converted to Judaism. Or as I now refer to it . . . Chewdaism. He's Chewish. But he wasn't born Chewish. As we all know, he was born a fur ball. And truth be told, Chewie is so hairy that no one really knows if he was circumcised or not.

Some of you may have noticed that Chewie is not wearing his yarmulke today. Unfortunately, when I was dressing him this morning for his big day, he thought it was a chew toy, so apologies for that.

Anyway, I just want to say I'm really proud of you, Chewie. No doubt you're going to get a lot of similar gifts: lint rollers, Dustbusters, manscaping trimmers. But it's the thought, and the hair removal, that counts, right? We've been through a lot together, and it makes me so happy that you've discovered this wonderful faith to help guide you through the universe.

Let's all raise our glasses and say mazel tov! Chewie, I love ya, and you can stick your head out the window of my spaceship anytime.

HOMER SIMPSON'S GRADUATION TOAST TO BART SIMPSON

Attention, everyone . . . I'd like to say a few words.
My name is Homer Simpson, and I'm Bart's father,
despite what that last DNA test said. Last time I buy
one of those kits at the Dollar Tree. And, no, Marge
didn't tell me to do this. In fact, she specifically
said not to say anything. But I rarely make the
right choice.

Thank you all for coming. And thank you to Moe for
letting us have Bart's high school graduation party in
his bar. The complimentary pretzels are on me.

I want to make a toast. Mmm, toast. Anyway, what
can I say about my son? No, seriously, I'm asking
you. I don't know what to say. This wouldn't be so
hard if it were Lisa. She's so easy to compliment.
I could say that she's the smartest person I know,
and I know exactly seventeen people. Or I could say
that she's an amazing saxophone player. She also
plays the accordion, but I don't know if she's any
good, because the accordion sounds horrible either
way. Or I could talk about how Lisa is the youngest

member of Mensa . . . which I think stands for Men of San Antonio. So, pretty impressive for a girl to get into that group. I could go on and on, but we're not here just to talk about Lisa. I have to talk about Bart. I guess I'll just fake it like I do at the power plant.

Bart, I can't believe you graduated high school. It seems like you were in the fourth grade for thirty-five years. But that can't be right, because you're only eighteen. I guess that's why I'm not a number scientist.

I should probably give you some advice. Stay in school. Wait, you're done with school. So don't stay in school. Stay out of school.

What other fatherly advice can I give you? Don't have kids. They're very expensive.

Oh, I thought of one of those similes. Life is like a box of doughnuts. Actually, no, it's not, because I love doughnuts. And I'm not too crazy about life. Unless I'm eating a doughnut. Mmm, doughnuts.

Bart, I know we've had our differences. I'm sorry for all the times I choked you by your neck. It's a good

thing you never called Child Protective Services.
If you had, I would've wrung your neck.

So, everyone, raise your glasses. D'oh! I don't wear
glasses. I guess I'll just hold up my drink. To my boy,
Bart! Congratulations. I'm proud of you, and I love
you very much.

In Closing

You did it!
Bravo. You made
the journey.
Beautifully too!

There are a lot of reasons to feel good after your speech:

- At least it's over!

- You didn't throw up. (We hope.)

- The hot bridesmaid asked for your number.

- Her father, who once said he never liked you, just invited you to play golf at his country club.

- The manager of the venue offered you a future friends-and-family discount.

- Everyone is complimenting what you wrote, making you even madder that you got a D in creative writing.

- The hot groomsman asked for your number.

- You can watch the bride's inebriated aunt try to do the Chicken Dance.

- You get to watch the person following you bomb!

We hope our book brought you success. If it helped just one person give a funny speech, well, that's pretty low returns, and now we're sad.

Congratulations! We'll see you out on the speech circuit! Make it so good, nobody wants to follow you. Including us!

Acknowledgments

To Olivia Roberts, our fearless millennial editor, whose guidance was invaluable. Thank you! And to Steve Fisher, the superagent who made it all happen.

Carol

Thanks to my pals Jon Macks, Cathy Rath, and Lynn Burkes. 🩶

Rick

My friend Brian Kiley: For your expert comedic touch.

My mom, dad, and sister: Thanks for laughing at things I've said over the years and giving me the confidence to pursue a career in comedy and writing.

My good friends: For asking me to speak at your weddings.

Our dogs, Teddy and Nilla: I'm not sure what I'm acknowledging them for, but my daughter would be upset if I don't since they are very much part of our family.

About the Authors

CAROL LEIFER is an Emmy Award winner who has written for such shows as *Hacks*, *Seinfeld*, *Curb Your Enthusiasm*, *Modern Family*, *Saturday Night Live*, *The Larry Sanders Show*, and ten Academy Awards. As a stand-up, Carol has appeared on *The Tonight Show*, HBO, Showtime, Comedy Central, and has made twenty-five appearances on *Late Night with David Letterman*. Her two previous books are *When You Lie About Your Age, the Terrorists Win* and *How to Succeed in Business Without Really Crying*. Carol is a popular speaker on the corporate/nonprofit circuit, delivering speeches for over one hundred organizations.

If you would like personal help with a speech, reach out through her website, carolleifer.com.

RICK MITCHELL is a five-time Emmy-winning writer/producer for *The Ellen DeGeneres Show*. He also spent years as a writer/producer for *TMZ on TV*, where he also made daily appearances hurling out jokes from the back of the room. As a stand-up, Rick has appeared on Fox's *Laughs* and has performed at many comedy clubs, including The Improv, Punchline San Francisco, and The Ice House. His two previous books are *The Great Gatsby* and *1984*. He didn't write those . . . he just read them.

If you would like personal help with a speech, reach out through his website, rickmitchell.com.

Photo by Innis Casey.